The Paras
Afghanistan

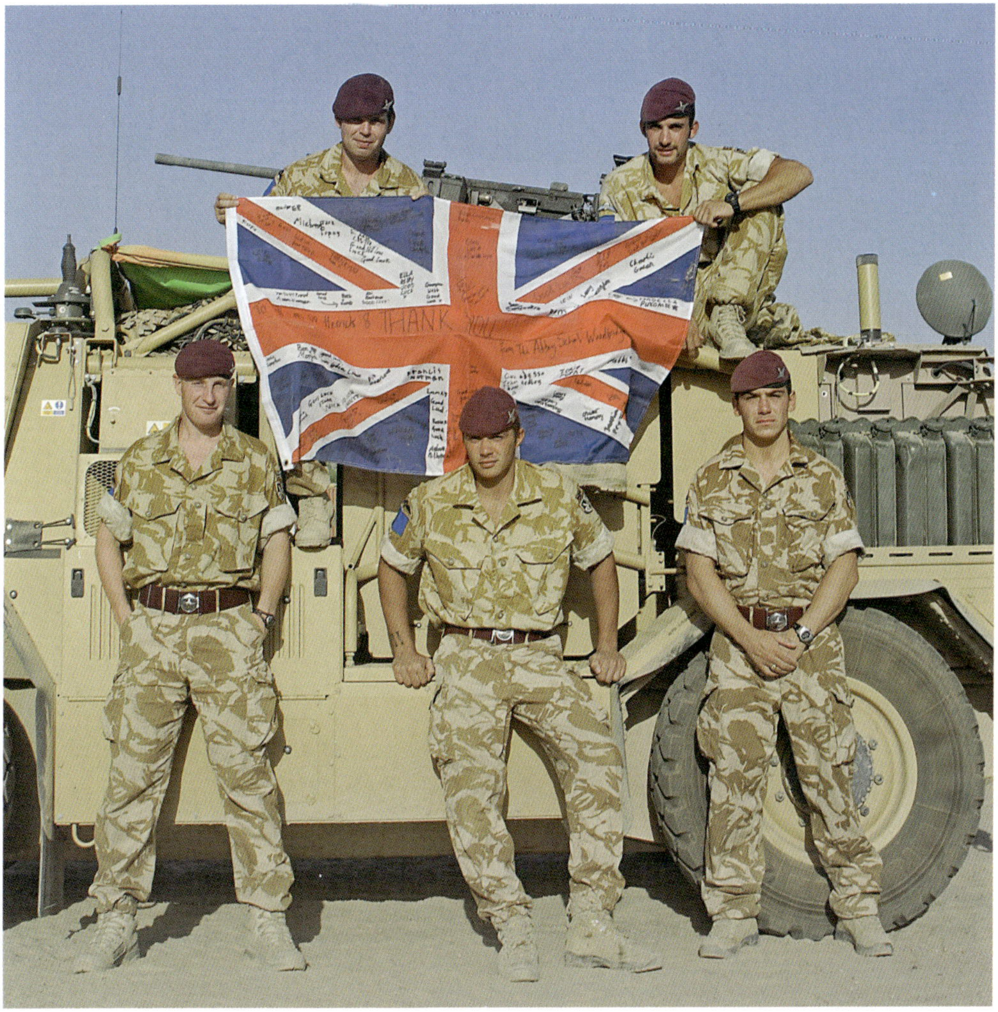

CRAIG ALLEN

Key Books

MODERN WARS SERIES, VOLUME 2

Front cover image: B Company 3 Para in Musa Qala.

Back cover image: D Company 2 Para operating from FOB Robertson.

Title page image: 2 Para Rover group photo at Sangin.

Contents page image: B Company 3 Para in Musa Qala.

Published by Key Books
An imprint of Key Publishing Ltd
PO Box 100
Stamford
Lincs, PE19 1XQ

www.keypublishing.com

The right of Craig Allen to be identified as the author of this book has been asserted in accordance with the Copyright, Designs and Patents Act 1988 Sections 77 and 78.

Copyright © Craig Allen, 2022

ISBN 978 1 80282 186 4

All rights reserved. Reproduction in whole or in part in any form whatsoever or by any means is strictly prohibited without the prior permission of the Publisher.

Typeset by SJmagic DESIGN SERVICES, India.

Contents

Prologue		4
A Note on Equipment		5
Chapter 1	**Preparation for Battle**	6
	Otterburn Live-firing	6
	OPTAG Training	9
	Tactical Training Kirkcudbright	9
Chapter 2	**2 Para**	13
	Fighting from the FOBs	13
	FOB Inkerman	13
	FOB Sangin	28
	FOB Gibraltar	33
	FOB Robertson	59
Chapter 3	**3 Para**	77
	Zabul	77
	Kandahar	84
	Musa Qala	94
	Kajaki Dam	116
End Game		128

Prologue

In early 2008, I was working as a contractor at Standard Life in Edinburgh and putting in time with the Army Reserve 4 Para at weekends. The office was not my natural environment, and I had little in common with my co-workers. In fact, the job was steadily grinding me down, and I would stare longingly out of the windows at pedestrians passing by. Then I heard that the Parachute Regiment was gearing up for another operational tour of Afghanistan. I had tried to join the previous tour in 2006 without success, but this time, I was determined to find a place. At 47 years of age, it would probably be my last hurrah and a final chance to return to operational soldiering. Handing in my ID card at the front desk, I was soon back in uniform again. With both 2 and 3 Para engaged in pre-operational training, I became a regular with the Permanent Range Teams working out of Otterburn. It was an easy commute from my Edinburgh home and got me back into the swing of things as I tramped across the field firing ranges. Upon mobilising, I joined other members of 4 Para for the OPTAG training package. This began at Wathgill Camp in Yorkshire, followed by live-firing at Hyth and Lydd Ranges in Kent. I requested a place as a frontline photographer, and, luckily for me, Regimental Colonel John Handford was familiar with my work and endorsed me. This was fortunate, as, given my age, I would otherwise have spent the entire tour in Camp Bastion

watch-keeping. As it was, I was able to join the Parachute Battalions in theatre as they confronted a resurgent Taliban in the fields and ditches of Helmand. This was to involve visiting all the frontline bases manned by 2 Para, along with several operations mounted by 3 Para, which operated in a 'Fire Force' role for the brigade.

A Note on Equipment

For the 2003 campaigns in Iraq, I still carried a film camera as backup, but by 2008, I was fully reliant on digital in the shape of the Nikon D200. It was a semi-pro model, thankfully well sealed against the elements, although the dust of Helmand still caused me a few issues. I had hoped to secure some photographic gear through the military, but this did not happen, so I fell back on my own camera and a couple of tried and tested lenses. These were a 28-105mm mid-range zoom partnered with a 70-300mm telephoto. Neither of these were professional models, but they stood up well to the tough conditions in Afghanistan. The Regiment later supplied me with one of the newer 28-200mm super-zooms, which was excellent. Sadly, it did not survive damage it received while I was jumping into ditches in Musa Qala, and I returned to my two old favourites. As digital cameras are totally reliant on rechargeable batteries, I was thankfully able to use power sources available at the FOBs or portable generators when on operations. For image storage and basic editing, I relied on a small ASUS notebook computer, which could fit handily into my daysack and was robust enough for use in the field. In the end, it was access to the battlefield and being in the right place at the right time that mattered more than the camera gear, and in that respect, I was lucky.

Chapter 1
Preparation for Battle

Otterburn Live-firing

It was said that the Battle of Waterloo was won on the playing fields of Eaton, and troops trained at Sennybridge in Wales prior to the Falklands War. In preparation for tours of Afghanistan, however, the Parachute Regiment chose Otterburn in Cumbria. This suited me very well, as this location happened to be only a couple of hours drive from my home in Edinburgh. I became a regular commuter to the wind-swept training area, spending my days in the field on range safety duties, a welcome change from office life. The rifle companies would shuttle through Otterburn, conducting a series of live-firing exercises by both day and night. They fired all their weapon systems and practised the tactics and manoeuvres they would use once deployed in Helmand. For me, this was a rewarding and enjoyable time, as I joined former colleagues to provide safety cover and got to work outdoors every day. It felt good to drop back into the routines of military life and feel that I was playing a useful role in the Regiment's preparations. The days spent tramping across the tussock grass and broken ground of Otterburn wearing 13kg of body armour also did wonders for my personal fitness.

The rifle companies rotated through a programme of live-firing exercises, building up to day and night attacks in conjunction with support weapons. These were conducted with the troops wearing Osprey body armour and carrying 'live scales' of ammunition that amounted to a considerable weight. Personal fitness is something akin to a religion in the Regiment, but it was still an exhausting business. It was clear that the additional loads were hampering the troops mobility, and things would be even tougher in the summer heat of Helmand. One new development, first used in Iraq in 2003, was the appearance of quad bikes, both as load carriers and to position forward observation teams and snipers. These rugged little machines were already a common sight on military training areas in the hands of local sheep farmers, so it is surprising that the army took so long to discover their usefulness.

The Permanent Range Team (PRT) gathers on a cold November 2007 morning in Otterburn, Cumbria.

Right: 'Contact' is initiated, and the troops lay down fire with their personal weapons.

Below: Simulated casualty evacuation. The nearest man is carrying the .338 sniper rifle.

Above left: A platoon sergeant rushes forward with the 51mm mortar; this could fire high-explosive illumination and smoke rounds.

Above right: The 5.56mm LMG (Light Machine Gun), seen here fitted with a SUSAT sight, was to provide useful extra firepower in Helmand.

Below: The 7.62mm GPMG (General Purpose Machine Gun), known as 'Gimpy' to the troops.

Colour Sergeant (CSgt) Thomson gives a lesson at Wathgill Camp, Catterick.

OPTAG Training

As I was mobilising from 4 Para, our own preparatory training was conducted at Catterick and Kirkcudbright, followed by an OPTAG (Operational Training and Advisory Group) package held at Hythe and Lydd. For the initial stages, I was mainly employed as an instructor, and for the live-firing at Kirkcudbright, I worked with the PRT. Returning to Hythe and Lydd brought back memories of Northern Ireland training from the past. While here, we benefited from the instructor's recent experience in Afghanistan. The subjects covered included everything from ambush drills to clearing an Afghan compound and dealing with mines and IEDs. It was all very useful stuff, and it concentrated everyone's minds on the challenges ahead. It was during this period that my own future employment firmed up after a meeting with Regimental Colonel John Handford. I would now be deploying as an official photographer to cover the Regiment's part in the coming operational tour of Helmand. This was not a completely new role for me, as I had operated as a media escort and photographer for the campaign in Iraq, back in 2003.

Tactical Training Kirkcudbright

The regular battalions completed their live-firing packages at Otterburn, but the 4 Para contingent headed to Kirkcudbright in Dumfries and Galloway. On the ranges here, they were able to practise section and platoon tactics, both blank and live, using all their weapon systems. Practice assaults were made using blanks, before switching to live ammunition. The training was conducted in full body armour and carrying realistic combat loads, which proved a good test of the soldiers' battle fitness. The training built up from pairs to section, and then finally full-blown platoon attacks with supporting fire from the GPMGs. This training was to hold the reservists in good stead once they deployed into theatre with their respective battalions.

Opposite: A GPMG gunner is on the start line with a 50-round belt loaded on the gun.

Above: A section reacts to coming under simulated attack.

Right: 'Keep low and move fast!' Note the Chorley grenade in his left hand.

Above left: Laying down suppressive fire. Note the ejected case in the air.

Above right: The Gun Group is called forward during one of the blank attacks.

Below: The troops advance past a relic from an earlier conflict.

Chapter 2
2 Para

Fighting from the FOBs

The Forward Operating Bases (FOBs) had been set up at the start of the campaign in Helmand in 2006, in order to establish a presence and dominate the ground. However, what happened instead was that they drew the resurgent Taliban onto British forces in a series of epic sieges, notably at Sangin and Musa Qala. Since then, the Taliban fighters were pushed back, and direct assaults on the FOBs had become rare, although stand-off attacks with heavy weapons were still a fairly regular occurrence, and the daily patrols into the surrounding Green Zone would inevitably bring contact with the enemy. These missions usually involved a company or company minus, as the Taliban were also operating in strength; as one commander succinctly put it to me, 'We don't want to get our arses kicked.' The reality was that there were simply never sufficient troops to dominate the ground properly, a situation only exacerbated by leave rotations, sickness and the inevitable casualties. The patrols went out day after day, week after week, in a cycle that became known as 'mowing the lawn'. With superior firepower provided by artillery and mortars based at the FOBs, and with air strikes on call, the soldiers invariably won the firefights. Nevertheless, the insurgents would still be there the next day, and so the cycle went on. The enemy consisted of hardcore Taliban troops supported by foreign fighters and a smattering of local farmers, the so-called 'dollar-a-day Taliban'. They could not hope to win a direct confrontation with well-armed Western troops, but they could certainly draw them into firefights and inflict casualties. The use of suicide bombers and the proliferation of IEDs only increased the threat to the frontline troops; this was asymmetric warfare at its most effective. The goal was always to wear down the resolve of Western troops, and as the Taliban liked to say, 'We had the watches, but they had the time.' The soundness of this tactic was to be proved correct in the chaotic withdrawal of Western troops from Kabul in the summer of 2021.

FOB Inkerman

In July 2008, Inkerman was to be my first experience of the FOBs that were strung out along the Helmand Valley. It had earned the nickname 'In-Coming', after coming under incessant attack by the insurgents. Thankfully, aggressive patrolling by the men of B Company 2 Para had driven the Taliban Mortar and RPG (rocket-propelled grenade) teams back. Despite this, patrols into the surrounding hinterland invariably provoked a response from the enemy. I recognised some familiar faces from amongst the company senior non-commissioned officers (SNCOs), and, from chatting with former colleagues, it was clear I had just missed a major bust-up with the enemy the day before. It seemed that this place was still very much active, and as one of the seniors so eloquently put it, 'Every time we go out, it's advance to ambush.' With the next patrol not due until the next day, I was able to a have a look around my new home for the next week and take some shots of the base. A 'stand to' by the Royal Artillery (RA) crews gave me a chance to photograph the 105mm Light Guns coming into action, although in the end they were not required to fire.

Above left: Washing clothes in the admin area outside – it was a constant battle to keep clean!

Above right: The 4 Platoon Orbat or Order of Battle Board.

Below: The veteran 105mm Light Gun was still the mainstay of the RA.

Above: Mail goes out on a resupply flight, providing a vital link with home.

Below: Queuing for the evening meal. Note the youthfulness of the soldiers.

The *Star Wars* Village

An early patrol involved a sweep through a local settlement that the troops had nicknamed the '*Star Wars* village'. The mission was in support of an Afghan National Army (ANA) callsign, and the young Para platoon commander (PC) confirmed they were expecting trouble. The village itself turned out to be close to the FOB and only a short walk in the fierce afternoon heat. The ANA patrol was already in place and travelling light as usual; their gunners were festooned with ammunition belts for their PKs. The place did indeed remind you of a *Star Wars* set, and the locals mostly kept out of sight, except for curious children. The Afghan troops set up a road-stop on the dusty track at the bottom of the settlement, while B Company provided cover from a convenient ditch. It did not take long for the insurgents to react, with a shot ringing out from the surrounding Green Zone. This got everyone searching the treeline for signs of the enemy, but things quickly settled down again. It was probably just a local farmer or 'dollar-a-day Taliban' member taking a pot shot. Before collapsing back to the FOB, the PC had an impromptu meeting with the ANA commander, while the platoon formed a loose cordon for protection.

Left: As troops leave the FOB in staggered file, note that everyone carries daysacks loaded with spare ammunition and extra water.

Opposite above: A view of the FOB, which was built up from an Afghan compound with HESCO defences.

Opposite below: A sniper pair set up a fire position with their powerful .338 rifle.

2 Para

Left: An ANA RPG (rocket-propelled grenade) gunner squats in the shade. Note the spare rockets in his backpack.

Below: A rifleman uses a convenient wall for cover; he has fitted a foregrip to his SA80A2.

Above: This para is armed with the 40mm UGL (underslung grenade launcher), which had an effective range of 300m.

Right: This section commander displays typical equipment, including commercial ammunition pouches, a daysack and a low-slung holster for the SIG Sauer 9mm pistol.

Above: The veteran 7.62mm GPMG, which was still the basis of platoon-level firepower.

Left: A GPMG gunner shoulders his weapon and heads back to the platoon lines.

6 Platoon Local Patrol

I joined 6 Platoon for another patrol into the local area the next afternoon; daily patrols were the bread and butter of the soldiers' life here. It began in the usual fashion, with radio checks and the troops readying their weapons in the loading bays. Then they were stepping off, staggering their exit from the camp gate. There seemed to be more people this time, and the PC questioned a couple of Afghan men through the interpreters. They looked for all the world like the Talibs that shot at us every day, and, for all we knew, they could have been.

The troops head for the loading bays; note the kneepads and bayonets tucked into MOLLE loops on the Osprey vests.

The platoon commander carries his spare ammunition in a shoulder bag; note the personal role radio (PRR) and drinking tube.

Left: The troops lead off across the barren ground surrounding the FOB.

Below: A GPMG gunner provides overwatch from the cover of a low wall.

Above: Chatting with a local elder; the interpreters were invaluable for this kind of thing.

Right: This rifleman carries a 66mm Light Anti-Tank Weapon (LAW) strapped to his daysack.

The gunners come in. Note the slings over one shoulder, which allows the gun to be deployed quickly.

Clearance Patrol

A first-light clearance patrol gave me another opportunity to get out on the ground after some suspicious digging had been reported near one of the sangers (a fortified position). It was ironic that an Afghan with a shovel was now almost as much of a threat as one wielding an AK, given the prevalence of IEDs. Early next morning, I piled into the back of a Pinzgauer with the specialist clearance team, and we headed out with the Fire Support Group riding shotgun in their Land Rover WMIKs (Weapons Mounted Installation Kits).

Dropping short of the suspected area, the search operators went to work with their Vallum probes, which are essentially modern versions of the World War Two mine detectors. It was slow, exacting work, and if anything suspicious was found, it was down to brushing away the sand, probing with a bayonet. At this point, people would naturally step back, not wanting to bother the soldier while he was working!

The WMIKs push out first, acting as a mobile screen.

The team begins to work their way to the site of the digging.

It is painstaking business to clear this well-used track.

Right: Taking a closer look. Everyone steps back, not wanting to bother the man while he is working!

Below: Using a bayonet as a probe is a classic technique.

Postscript: The company was gearing up for a major operation into the Green Zone, which I had planned to join, when I was suddenly recalled to Sangin for re-tasking. This was a disappointment for me at the time, and sadly, during the subsequent operation, the company at Inkerman took casualties in a major confrontation with the insurgents.

FOB Sangin
General
Sangin had a fearsome reputation, earned during 3 Para's first tour back in 2006, when it had been besieged by the Taliban. Fast forward to 2008 and things were a little more stable, with the sprawling base now home to 2 Para's headquarters, plus a rifle company of the Royal Irish Regiment. Initially, I found myself kicking my heels at Sangin waiting for a ride on a resupply flight up country to one of the FOBs. Life seemed fairly benign, with nightly briefings by the CO of 3 Para that reminded me of the 1600hr follies from Richard Herr's Vietnam book, *Dispatches*. The tone was uniformly downbeat, with a steady stream of casualty reports and little in the way of progress. With time on my hands, I photographed activity around camp that ranged from the mundane to the bizarre. As always, the troops were making the best of it, with improvised gyms and swimming trips to the nearby river. The latter was a welcome relief from the oppressive heat, and the guys had rigged up a surfboard to take advantage of the fast-flowing water. I chatted with some of the Provincial Reconstruction Team at mealtimes, and it seemed their rotations were being reduced to three months due to the fighting. It begged the question of what could be achieved in such a short tour, and I thought of the old colonial district officers who spent some 30 years in post, spoke the language and were intimate with all the local personalities.

Around Camp
As I was later to discover, Sangin was pretty typical of the FOBs in Helmand. The importance of Sangin was down to geography, in that it linked the provincial capital Lashkar Gah with northern Helmand and the UK bases further up the valley. Daily life for the troops stationed there was a round of patrolling and maintaining the FOB; the only things to look forward to were the resupply flights bringing mail from home and the mid-tour R&R. Living conditions were basic, and the food was mostly rice and noodles, along with meals the army cooks conjured up from ten-man ration packs. Despite the tough conditions, the soldiers were young and fit and used to living in the field, so soon adapted to this frontline existence. Well into my 40s at this point, I was not quite as robust, but a lifetime with the Royal Irish Regiment had prepared me for these challenges, and I made myself comfortable, taking over a small alcove where I pitched my camp bed.

The Enemy
In 2006, Sangin was effectively under siege, with both direct assaults from Taliban fighters and regular incoming fire from rockets and mortars. By 2008, things were a little different; greater firepower and aggressive patrolling pushed the insurgents back from the town. However, it remained an edgy and dangerous place to serve, walking down the main street always drew suspicious and hostile looks from the local Afghans. This is not surprising, as we brought the fighting with us and disrupted the burgeoning opium trade they relied on. After a week at the FOB, I did manage to get out on the ground with the Irish Rangers for a local operation. Taking over an abandoned compound about a klick (km) from the main base, they began patrolling the surrounding area. It did not take long for the enemy to show their hand, with the new patrol base (PB) subject to early-morning attack by RPGs and small arms fire. It was clear the Taliban had not gone away and still posed a lethal threat to UK forces. More than 100 British

soldiers and marines lost their lives in and around Sangin over the years, and it is a place that became synonymous with the fighting in Helmand. When US Marines took over in 2010, during the surge, they had an equally difficult experience, cementing its reputation as a nexus for the fighting.

Evidence of an earlier conflict can be seen in these Russian wrecks on the edge of town.

A mobile patrol is about to leave the base. These often came under attack from the insurgents.

Above left: Combat surfing in the fast-flowing Helmand River.

Above right: A forest of antennas sprout from Sangin's main command sanger.

Left: Quad bikes were useful for recovering helicopter loads.

Above left: A memorial to those who had fallen defending Sangin from the insurgents.

Above right: The outdoor gym saw plenty of use by the young paras.

Right: A patrol from the Royal Irish Rangers. The foreground man carries an SA80A2 with UGL fitted.

Keeping alert during a patrol into the local area. The point man carries a 5.56mm LMG with ACOG.

The Royal Irish Rangers search houses. Note the clover leaf patches on the helmets.

Clearance patrols go out in the wake of the attack on the PB.

FOB Gibraltar

After my stay in Sangin, I was able to move to Camp Bastion, with its handy media facilities and flight line. This was to make my life much easier over the coming months, as I could catch a resupply flight out to the FOBs and rest up and edit material at Bastion between jobs. At Inkerman, I had missed the opportunity to cover a major operation into the Green Zone that had resulted in contact with the enemy. As the old saying goes, 'be careful what you wish for', and my next deployment to FOB Gibraltar was to offer plenty of opportunities to get close to the action. The troops at Gibraltar were facing attacks from a large and determined group of insurgents and were to be re-enforced by elements from 3 Para. I was able to find space on one of the Chinook flights taking them into the base, where, with the 3 Para incoming, the garrison could sally forth to take on the Taliban.

Like Inkerman, the FOB had developed organically, starting from an original mudbrick compound and later protected and extended by HESCO defences and dotted with numerous sangers. The top half of the camp was crowded with living shelters and contained the command post (CP) and cookhouse. The lower half more resembled a construction site and was dotted with shipping containers, boxes of spare parts and parked vehicles. A small forest of antennas sprang from the roof of the CP, along with a tattered Union Jack. Gibraltar looked exactly like what it was – a far-flung outpost in a faraway war.

Above: The pits for the 81mm mortars, a vital component of any FOB.

Left: Volleyball was a popular off-duty pastime for the troops.

Above left: Satellite phones were a vital link with home, and the soldiers were issued pre-paid cards to use them.

Above right: Sleeping arrangements were basic: a camp cot and pod with mosquito netting. The sleeping pods were everywhere, and, as the Taliban had been pushed back, it was safe to sleep outside.

Below: The washing area with classic stove pipe boilers for hot water.

Above left: One of the sangers is draped in camouflage netting. The rubber traps in the foreground appear to be from a BV 206.

Above right: The company CP. Note the dish for satellite communications.

Left: Enjoying dinner was one of the few daily pleasures, although the diet was mainly composed of ten-man ration packs.

Above left: The C Company operations room was manned 24 hours a day.

Above right: The outdoor shower stalls, which were used with solar shower bags.

Dawn Patrol

We were awake before dawn, and we struggled into our gear as the first light of dawn brushed the horizon. The 2 Para boys looked visibly battle-worn after months of living on hard rations and mounting regular patrols against the Taliban. Despite this, they were determined to take the fight to the enemy, their defence now bolstered by extra numbers from 3 Para. The men were all business as they made their preparations, stubbing out last-minute cigarettes and loading up their weapons. The radios buzzed into life, and I tucked in behind the command group as we left the FOB. Outside, there was little sign of activity, except for a couple of bearded elders, and the men shook out into staggered file and followed a track along the edge of the Green Zone. Reaching some abandoned compounds, the PC climbed a roof to survey the ground, which soon elicited a flurry of shots followed by a long burst of automatic fire – the game was on!

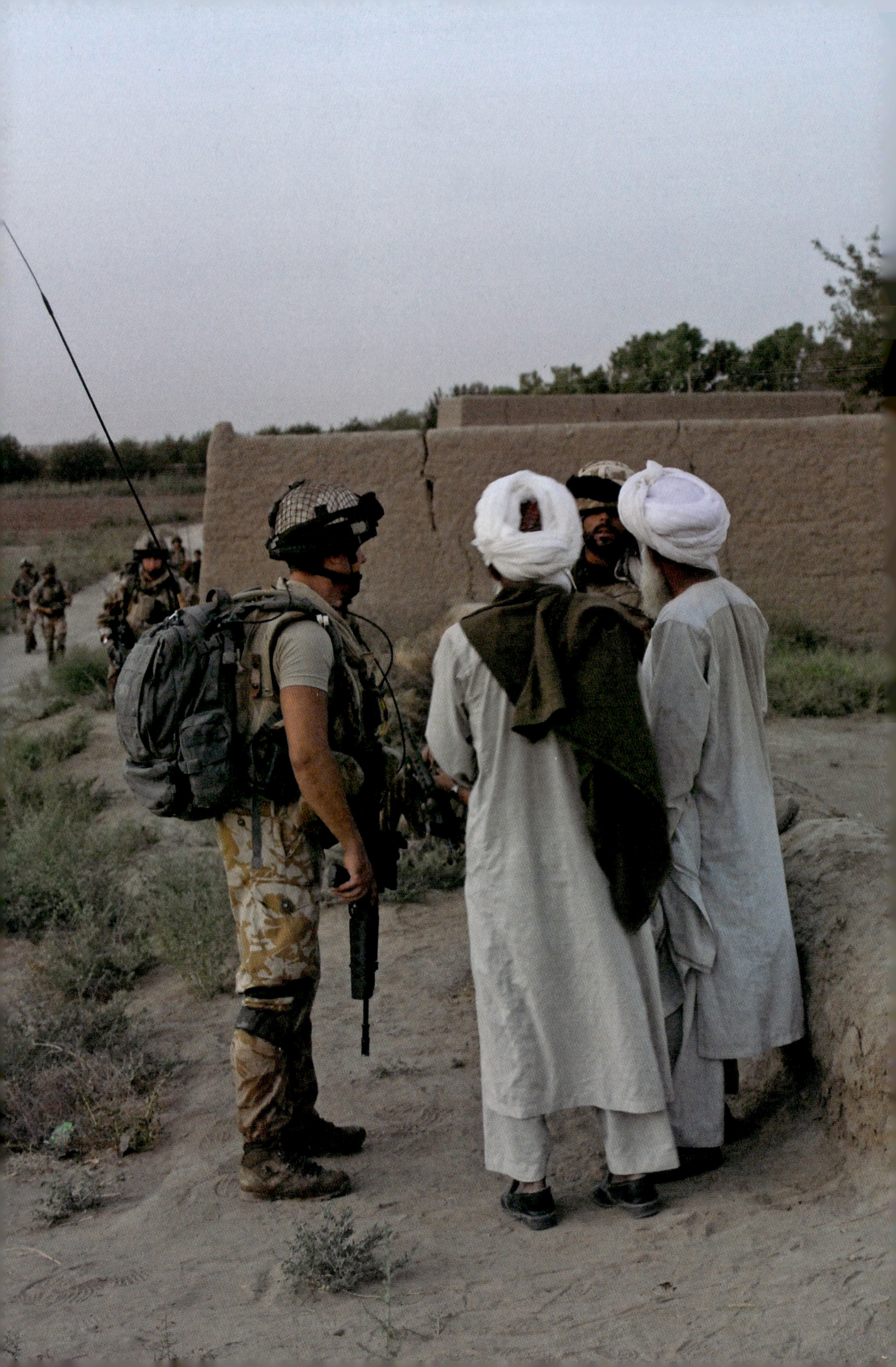

Opposite: The officer commanding (OC) is chatting with a couple of local elders through an interpreter.

Right: This para carries a Swedish-designed AT4 rocket launcher.

Below: The diminutive Minimi 5.56mm LMG was a welcome boost to firepower.

Above: Meeting up with an ANA callsign from the local patrol base.

Left: The missiles for the Javelin made for a substantial load.

Right: Half of a bar mine was carried for breaching the thick compound walls.

Below: On the move! Note that the second soldier is wearing Disruptive Pattern Material (DPM), which offered better camouflage in the verdant Green Zone.

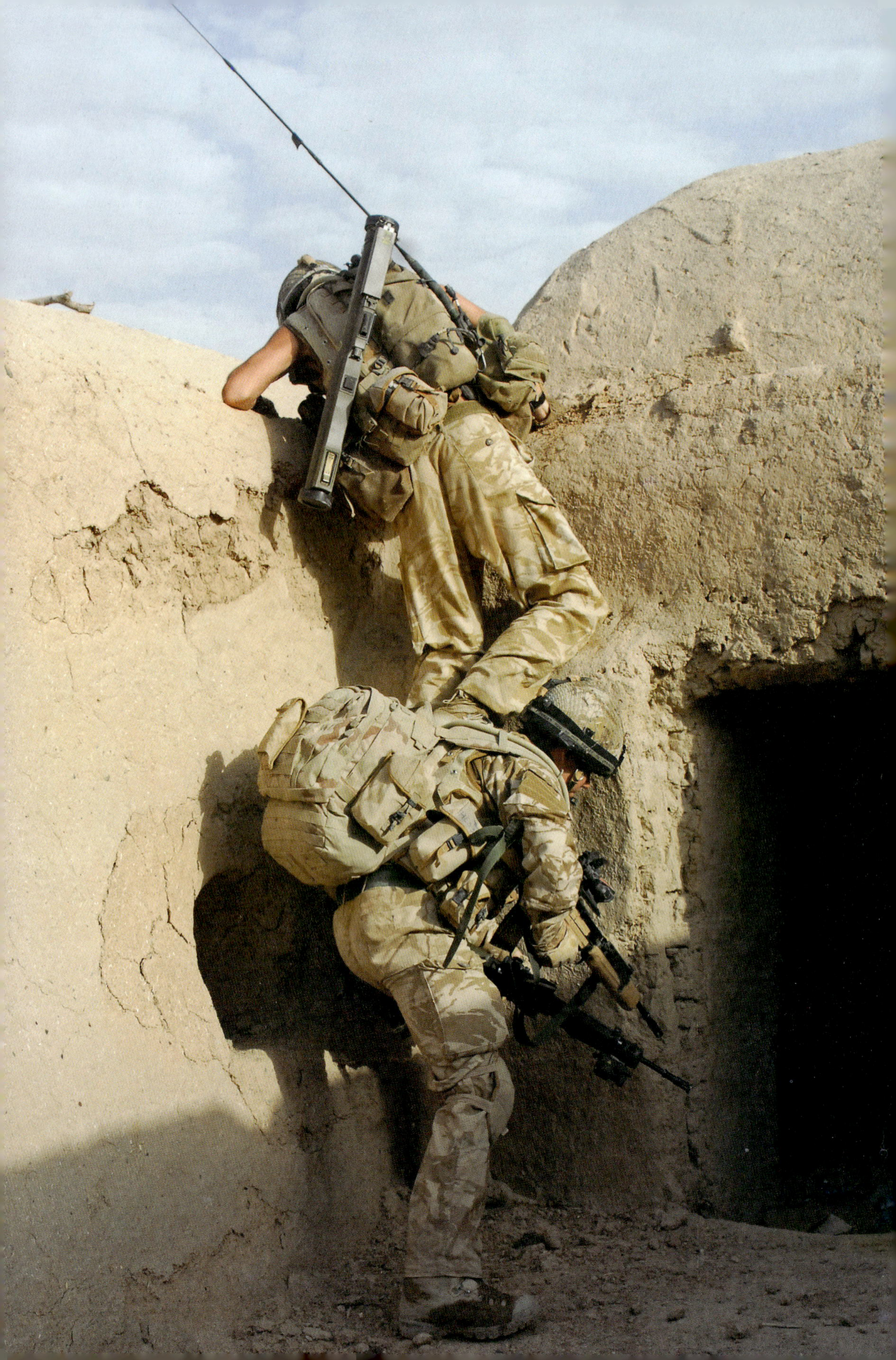

Follow Up

After the initial contact, a cat-and-mouse game ensued as the company attempted to outflank the Taliban fighters that were constantly changing position. The maze of fields and ditches and the thick vegetation favoured the insurgents who knew the ground intimately. Abandoned compounds became temporary fighting bases for both sides, and the ditches made useful trenches. As was so often the case, the result of the action was inconclusive, with the illusive enemy withdrawing to fight another day.

Opposite: The PC climbs onto the roof of an abandoned compound to spy on the land.

Right: Moving up. It is hard to move fast if you are the ECM man!

Left: The irrigation ditches offer covered approaches.

Below: A sniper seeks out the enemy through his scope. His weapon was effective far beyond the range of the SA80s.

A rifleman uses a fold in the ground for a fire position.

Crossing open ground to the next group of compounds; this is always a tense moment.

Left: **This LMG gunner is keeping a sharp eye out for the enemy.**

Below: **The troops use their ACOGs to scan the ground for the enemy.**

A sniper covers the ground with his 7.62mm L96, which is fitted with a Schmidt & Bender scope.

The 66mm LAW (Light Anti-Tank Weapon). This was an older weapon system that was put back into production and was popular with the troops.

Advance to Ambush

With the company mounting another fighting patrol into the Green Zone, I prepped my gear and joined the troops at the loading bays. It was early morning and we had not gone far when the ICOM Radio Scanner warned of the enemy manoeuvring into position ahead of us. The troops called this 'advance to ambush', and true to form, we were part way across a muddy field when an avalanche of automatic fire washed over us. Everyone immediately sprinted for the nearby tree line and hugged the dirt before returning fire. Thankfully, most of the enemy rounds went high, cutting through the foliage close above our heads. Then the air was split by the sudden 'woosh' of an incoming RPG round, which thankfully burst without causing casualties. The fire continued to come in thick and heavy, and initially mortar support was denied because of the close proximity of occupied dwellings. During a brief lull, we managed to move forward to a water-filled ditch that offered better cover. The platoon sergeant then began directing fire from the GPMGs to suppress the enemy fire. Despite this, the rounds were still zipping in like angry bees. The man next to me unslung and extended a Light Anti-Structures Missile (LASM) before launching it at the enemy in a cloud of smoke. I had come to cover the fighting, and here it was right in front of me.

Below left: This sniper carries a 7.62mm L96, which was handier to use in the close country of the Green Zone.

Below right: A para wearing a typical combat load, including a holstered 9mm SIG and a slung LAW.

Above: A view of FOB Gibraltar from outside the wire.

Right: The Javelin man doubles forward, despite his cumbersome load.

Left: The enemy could be behind any corner.

Below: 'Get some rounds down!' A ditch is as good as a trench in a firefight.

Above: The sniper identifies his target and takes the shot.

Right and below: Time for the LASM. The firer extends the launcher, aims and fires, then disappears in a cloud of smoke.

Things appear to have quietened down as the troops make their way back to Gibraltar.

Time for a group picture now that it is all over for another day.

Postscript: Eventually, the mortars and artillery were given 'weapons free', and supporting fire came raining in from the FOB and crashed down onto the Taliban positions. This put an end to things, with the insurgents rapidly withdrawing as the troops followed up. As was so often the case with these engagements, the results were inconclusive, but at least we suffered no casualties, despite the weight of fire directed against us.

Combat Logistic Patrol

Although some supplies did come in by air, the shortage of helicopters and the weight of some combat supplies meant that road convoys were vital to maintaining the FOBs. This was the job of the Combat Logistic Patrols (CLP) mounted from Bastion, and they brought fuel, ammunition and vital spares. With just such a resupply mission inbound, I joined a clearance patrol along the Main Supply Route (MSR) to help clear the way. This was a similar mission to the one I had covered at Inkerman, but this time it was the route itself that was priority. When the CPL eventually thundered past, I reflected that there can have been few more dangerous jobs that battle summer than driving a fuel or ammunition truck around Helmand.

The Vallum operators begin the route clearance using their probes.

Left: Checking out a suspicious reading from the Vallum probe.

Below: The route was also heavily used by the local population.

Above left: Checking for anything out of the ordinary was painstaking work.

Above right: This Vallum man still carries his SA80A2 with UGL, in case of trouble.

Right: The main sanger of the ANA PB.

Left: **If anything, the ANA living conditions are even more basic than the FOB.**

Below: **A huge armoured fuel tanker emerges from the dust.**

Above: An up-armoured M113 armoured personnel carrier (APC) provides protection for the CLP.

Right: ANA soldiers are equipped with US-supplied M16A2 5.56mm rifles and ballistic helmets.

Time for a quick group photograph.

The fuel trucks pump their cargo into the FOBs storage tanks.

Postscript: The deployment to Gibraltar brought me face to face with the sharp end of the campaign, and it gave me a clearer insight into the nature of the fighting. There were estimated to be up to 125 Taliban surrounding the FOB, including Pakistanis and hardened Chechen fighters. The fighting itself had been on a different level to anything I had experienced before, and, having accompanied them into action, I was full of admiration for the mettle of the troops.

FOB Robertson

FOB Robinson was the last of the 2 Para bases that I would cover, and it was occupied by D Company, who I had worked with during the build-up training in the UK. The OC, Major Rigby, was happy to have me on board, and I was billeted with 'Thomo', a Falklands vet and an old colleague from 4 Para. The FOB itself was larger than most and had originally been an American-manned base. In fact, there was still a US presence in the form of a Ranger unit housed in a side camp. As well as D Company, the FOB was home to a squadron of CVRTs (Combat Vehicle Reconnaissance Tracked) from the Royal Scots Dragoon Guards and an RA detachment equipped with a Guided Multiple Launch Rocket System (GMLRS). There was a substantial tented dining area complete with satellite TV, and the food was a little better than the usual FOB fare. I soon settled in and had the use of an ISO container with its own power source for my editing, which was a bonus.

The busy helicopter landing ground at FOB Robertson.

The GMLRS could launch its 12 rockets either singly or in salvoes. They were famously capable of taking out a grid and it was often simply too powerful to use in populated areas.

Supply parachutes made useful awnings for the troops' accommodation.

A sanger constructed from HESCO bastions and sandbags.

Dropping off stores from the quad bike and trailer.

Royal Scots Dragoon Guards' CVRTs, these veteran recce vehicles found a new lease of life in Afghanistan.

The Scimitar 2 featured a larger hull and upgraded power pack, while the potent 30mm Rarden cannon was retained as its main armament.

A view of the FOB from outside the wire.

The tented dining area even featured a satellite TV for the troops.

The Mi-8 comes in with an underslung load.

Local Patrol
My first patrol from the FOB involved a visit to a compound in the nearby 'Millionaires Row', which housed the wealthier Afghans. After this, the company would mount interdiction and presence patrols into the local area before retiring to an ANA PB for the night. It was an early start and the compound turned out to be situated close to the main base. The OC was soon holding an impromptu 'Shura' (an Afghan term for a meeting) with the village head man via the interpreter. The troops then moved down to the lower part of the settlement before crossing into open desert to reach the security of the ANA PB perched on a nearby hill.

This man displays typical patrol gear. Note the forward handgrip attached to his rifle.

Left: **The hefty 338-calibre sniper rifle was not the handiest weapon for patrolling.**

Below: **This man's unfeasibly large backpack holds the Command Launch Unit (CLU) for the Javelin.**

Above: Crossing what passes for a road in Helmand. Note the taxis in the background.

Right: Reaching our objective: the ANA PB.

Above left: A chance to get out of the Osprey, for a while at least.

Above right: This rifleman carries a 51mm mortar tube in his daysack.

ANA Patrol Base

The plan was to sit out the heat of the day at the ANA PB, and the troops soon made themselves busy constructing improvised shelters. Some unused HESCO baskets came in useful, while an old cargo chute was turned into a 'para tipi' to afford some welcome shade. Luckily, the CVRTs had brought in extra water and rations so we were able to make cups of tea and heat some food. The ANA troops manning the PB were mostly from the Hazara tribal group, historically discriminated against in Afghan society. The military offered new opportunities, and they had joined the ANA in significant numbers. They seemed a happy bunch, but played their music incessantly, which kept us awake half that night. The company was not idle in the hours of darkness and sent out an ambush patrol, but there was no contact with the enemy.

These unused HESCO baskets provide ready-made shelters – 'improvise and overcome'.

The tipi provides some shelter from the baking heat as the troops relax in the shade.

Above left: An ANA soldier with his US-supplied M16A2.

Above right: The Afghan national flag flies over the PB.

Below: The company moves in staggered file, with the outline of the FOB visible in the distance.

The corner sanger is perched on a hill.

FISH – Fighting in Someone's House

FISH may not have been an official army acronym, but it amply summed up the practice of taking over a compound as a fighting base. It was a tactic practised both by ourselves and the Taliban, with the unfortunate Afghan civilians caught in the middle. The occupants would usually just go to a neighbour or relative until the fighting blew over. Afterwards, a claim for damages made at the FOB might illicit some useful cash for repairs. In fact, these mudbrick dwellings were so sturdily built that even large-calibre weapons made little impression. It took powerful explosives or bar mines to actually breach their thick, hard-baked walls. The next operation would involve occupying a couple of compounds on the edge of the Green Zone in an effort to draw out the enemy fighters. On the face of it, the prospect of acting as a tethered goat did not sound all that appealing, but at least we would have the support of the gun-line from Inkerman. Determined not to be 'left out of battle', I put my reservations to one side and started packing my gear.

Left: The briefing session for the up-coming operation into the Green Zone.

Below: The barren nature of much of Helmand is clear from this image.

Closing up on the target compounds whilst being trailed by a local hound.

Establishing fire positions on the roof.

Left: Something's caught the sentry's eye, but so far things remain quiet.

Below: Time for a ration pack boil-in-the-bag meal now that the tension is off.

A grey-bearded elder speaks to the OC; doubtless there are complaints about damage to crops and buildings. These simple farmers were caught between us and the Taliban.

The veteran CVRTs had received a makeover for this campaign and operated as mobile fire support.

This Spartan APC carried the IED clearance team. Note the anti-RPG screens.

A quick group photograph before the men disperse.

Postscript: The mission was deemed a success as intelligence reports claimed the supporting fire from the 105mm Light Guns had inflicted casualties including a Taliban commander. All well and good, but you could guarantee the insurgents would still be there the next time we ventured out. They seemed well able to soak up their casualties, whereas the regular convoys through Wootton Bassett were increasingly raising questions at home.

Chapter 3
3 Para

Zabul

For my first major operation early in June, I joined B Company 3 Para for a trip to the mountainous Zabul Province, close to the Pakistani border. This was a favourite rest and transit area for Taliban fighters heading for Helmand. The aim of the mission was to interdict some of this traffic and to gauge the scale of the enemy presence. In the event, we were not to be disappointed, as, after a couple of days of local patrolling, the peace was shattered by a complex attack on our patrol base. This was initiated by an RPG attack over our compound, followed by a stand-off attack on the observation post (OP) on a nearby hill. I was out on patrol at the time, and we also came under fire from an HMG, probably a Russian-made Dushka. A few days later, the company mounted a heli-assault into an area some 12km to our north. The twin villages here were suspected to hold Taliban, and sure enough, we soon found ourselves in a firefight with the insurgents. The single mortar tube we had brought with us was soon in action, suppressing the enemy positions. Having won the firefight, we were faced with a long walk home, as the Chinooks were not available to extract us. A couple of days later, I caught a resupply flight back to Kandahar Airfield (KAF), 3 Para's home base. My time in the mountains had been a steep learning curve, but I had captured some useful images and would be better prepared next time.

Helicopter Loading Drills

Practice drills were carried out on the pan at KAF with the Dutch helicopter crews to ensure all the troops and equipment could be loaded smoothly. The Dutch squadron supported 3 Para throughout most of the tour and helped make up for the shortage of RAF transport helicopters. The Chinook was the real workhorse of the campaign, and their numbers and availability essentially dictated what could be achieved.

Practising making a swift exit to minimise the Chinooks time on the ground.

A quad bike powers off the ramp.

Unloading quickly was essential, as the helicopters were vulnerable on the ground.

Arrival

The flight offered spectacular views of the surrounding mountains as we climbed to reach our hilltop landing zone (LZ). The troops were soon running off the ramps and fanning out in a protective screen. The mortarmen, meanwhile, began setting up their tubes on the edge of the LZ to provide cover for the company. Our destination, a small settlement surrounded by orchards, was close by up a steep track. The company was soon moving off to occupy one of the compounds, our home for the duration of the operation.

Above left: Collecting ammunition for the 81mm mortars.

Above right: Setting up the mortars at the edge of the LZ.

Right: A Chinook arrives with an underslung load of supplies.

Setting up a GPMG SF (Sustained Fire) for point defence of the patrol base.

'Old faithful' – the 7.62mm GPMG is always a favourite with the Regiment.

Right: 'Bedding in' the 81mm mortar to stabilise the baseplate and improve accuracy.

Below: Poncho shelters were set up behind the compound's thick perimeter wall.

Above left: This LMG gunner illustrates the diminutive size of the 5.56mm Minimi with its short 13.7mm barrel.

Above right: Trudging up the hill with supplies for the OP manned by the Patrols Platoon.

Below: Sanger position at the OP. Note the suppressor that is fitted to the L115A1 sniper rifle.

The H&K 40mm GMG (Grenade Machine Gun) could throw its explosive rounds out to a range of 1,500m.

Running for a Chinook flight back to KAF.

A door gunner mans his 7.62mm GPMG in the Dutch Chinook.

Postscript: I initially found myself struggling with the weight of all my equipment, and I put this down to the fact I was twice the age of most of the 3 Para lads. However, I later discovered we were, in fact, operating at an elevation of some 4,000ft, and most had felt the effects of the altitude. Meanwhile, my issue desert boots had left me footsore on the long extraction march. I later purchased a pair of lightweight trekking boots at the KAF Post Exchange (PX) and wore these for the rest of the tour.

Kandahar

A dramatic prison break mounted against Kandahar's central jail had freed some 400 Taliban fighters who had quickly dispersed. B Company 3 Para were rapidly flown in from Zabul to stabilise the situation but were only to cover the first 24 hours. With A Company about to mount a RIP (Relief in Place) in order to replace them, I took the opportunity to cover the mission into the city. The aim was to provide security and reassurance to the civil population. The company would be housed in the city's football and sports stadium. The stadium had a somewhat sinister reputation, as the Taliban had once used it for public executions. Nevertheless, it was close to the city centre, and the football pitch offered a ready-made landing ground. Operating in city streets that busy with traffic was to prove a complete contrast to Zabul and the mountains. It was a reminder that Afghanistan also boasted bustling cities as well as the rural environments and deserts we were more familiar with.

Early Patrols

The sports stadium proved to be an ideal base with plenty of space to house the troops. It was also handy for mounting foot patrols into the city, where the locals seemed generally friendly. We arrived in darkness to relieve B Company, and I joined one of the early morning patrols to get my first look at the city. It seemed strange to be back in an urban environment, and with the road-stops and busy streets, it reminded me of my days in Northern Ireland. The people appeared better dressed and more prosperous than the poor farmers we normally dealt with. We passed through affluent neighbourhoods with their private security guards. This area also hosted the headquarters of various UN agencies and NGOs. Meanwhile, on the outskirts of the city, refugees displaced by the fighting lived a precarious existence in their shanty dwellings.

It was a novelty to be out on busy city streets.

Engaging with the locals. They seemed pleased to see us in the wake of the prison break.

Patrolling the poorer districts on the edge of town, home to refugees from the countryside.

Above: Carrying out a framework patrol to show a presence.

Below left: These ditches were basically open sewers, so I found another place to cross.

Below right: The GPMG seems a little too much gun for these street patrols.

The Sports Stadium

Upon occupying the stadium, the company took over several fortified positions on the roof, which gave excellent observation over the city. The well-kept playing field served as a ready-made LZ for the Chinooks bringing in supplies. The company mounted regular foot patrols into the city in order to reassure the population. These were, for the most part, uneventful, despite a couple of incidents with vehicles failing to stop at checkpoints. It gradually became apparent that, with the escaped insurgents having flown the coup, there was little reason to stay.

Above left: This .50cal in position on the stadium roof dominates the approaches to the city.

Above right: Two essential pieces of operational equipment: the SA80A2 rifle and flip-flops.

Left: This shot illustrates the impressive bulk of the Chinook, which has a long history stretching back to the Vietnam War.

An A Company callsign sets off on another patrol into the city.

The approaches to the stadium were protected with razor wire.

The ANA started mounting joint patrols and did not like to carry too much, as you can see.

Winding Down
After a few days, it became clear that we were no longer serving a real propose, and the CO turned up to assess the situation himself. After accompanying one of the foot patrols, he made the decision to withdraw, and the company set about packing up. The Canadians were to take over the security of the city, and a visit was arranged to the ANA commander to confirm the handover. This involved an exchange of flags, and the OC found himself being interviewed for Afghan television. It had been an interesting interlude, but, with another major operation brewing, it was time to return to KAF.

A platoon group picture on the stadium benches.

A Canadian Bison Armoured Personnel Carrier (APC), which was to escort us to the ANA headquarters.

The ANA turned out the guard for our benefit.

The OC finds himself being interviewed for Afghan television.

Above: An exchange of flags marks the handover of security for the city.

Right: Well, it is a football pitch after all!

Musa Qala

The next operation in 2008 would take B Company 3 Para to Musa Qala, which had been a nexus for the fighting during the 2006 tour. Back then, a mixed force from 3 Para and the Royal Irish Rangers had held off waves of insurgents in a latter day Rorke's Drift. As we were to discover, although the District Centre (DC) was no longer under direct attack, the Taliban were still present in some strength in the surrounding Green Zone. The aim of the mission was to draw out insurgents and distract them from a major operation being planned for Kajaki. In this, we certainly succeeded with numerous clashes with a determined enemy who proved more than happy to oblige us. Thankfully, the men under their aggressive commander, Major Stuart McDonald, were more than up to the task and fought toe to toe with the insurgents.

Infill

The move to Musa Qala began with a shuttle flight from KAF to Bastion by a C130 Hercules, then an overnight stay in the RSOI (Reception Staging and Onward Integration) blocks before flat beds ferried the troops down to the flight line. Chinooks then carried the company forward to FOB Edinburgh, which was manned by the jocks of the Royal Regiment of Scotland. From here, the troops were transported for the final leg to Musa Qala by Mastiffs, the huge armoured personnel carriers. Allegedly, these beasts were bulletproof even against powerful IEDs, though I still did not relish the 45-minute road move. Thankfully, the journey passed uneventfully, and we were soon deposited at the sprawling base that had grown up around the DC's building. We had been allocated an area of half-ruined compounds within the perimeter, where the men set up their pods and settled in for the night.

The troops load their kit onto flat beds for the short trip down to Bastion's flight line.

Above: The anti-tank men load up with their bulky Javelin missiles.

Right: The crew chief perches on the ramp of the Chinook for the fly in.

The Paras in Afghanistan

Mastiffs: these huge beasts were our transport for the last leg into Musa Qala.

The Mastiffs were surprisingly cramped inside; the roof hatch is for the .50cal gunner.

The DC at Musa Qala, surrounded by HESCO Bastion defences.

Patrol to the Patrol Base

The first part of the mission involved a foot move from Musa Qala to an ANA patrol base several klicks away on the edge of the Green Zone. This seemed simple enough, but the reality was to prove rather more testing. I had heard the thriving marketplace here being discussed as a sign of local development. Seeing the place first-hand exposed the disconnect between the hype and the reality on the ground. In fact, it was a sorry-looking affair and the whole place had a dystopian feel to it, scattered with the wrecks of shattered vehicles. Climbing up from the riverbank, we were soon into the usual maze of ditches, fields and compounds. It did not take long for the insurgents to react to our presence with a series of contacts that drew us deeper into the Green Zone. It was a cat-and-mouse game fought from compound to compound. As one fight would fizzle out, we would be engaged from another direction. What was planned as a simple move to our new patrol base soon became a long and drawn-out battle with the insurgents.

Left: Heading down to the lower camp, ready for the move.

Below: The dystopian sight that greeted us on the outskirts of town.

A typical image of the Green Zone, with its fields, ditches and compounds.

This man carries an infantry ladder, a vital piece of kit for fighting in the Green Zone.

The company rapidly advances, attempting to outflank the enemy fire position.

A sniper uses a ditch for cover. He has removed his helmet to enable him to get his eye to the scope.

Above left: The ECM man eases his load.

Above right: A sniper carries a 7.62mm L96. This weapon was better suited to the short engagement ranges in the Green Zone.

Below: The handler and her search dog. Note that she is armed with the curious-looking SA80 carbine.

Running Fight

The day was turning into a prolonged fight with the insurgents as they steadily retreated ahead of us. Following up through the maze of fields and ditches was an exhausting business, and the compounds became fighting positions for both sides. As the day waned, and the light began to go, it was time to retrace our steps towards our original destination. Meanwhile, a group of insurgents had manoeuvred into position between us and the patrol base. Our lead platoon was then met with a hail of fire as it crossed open ground, leaving myself and the following sections pinned behind an earth embankment. This time, however, the enemy location could be clearly identified, and supporting fire was quickly called in. Mortar rounds and 105mm shells were soon landing amongst the Taliban positions to the delight of the troops. The company was then able to move off safely as the rounds continued to roar in, bursting in the opposite tree line in a deadly firework display. We eventually reached the PB, tired after some 15 hours on the go, which included a series of running contacts with the enemy.

Left: A rifleman engages the enemy in the opposite tree line. Note the ejected case.

Below: Breaking into a suspect compound that may harbour enemy fighters.

Above left: The troops gain access and begin searching the compound for signs of the enemy.

Above right: Climbing a wall to get 'eyes on' the enemy positions.

Below: Clearing yet another suspect compound.

This compound roof provides a good observation position.

Pinned behind an earth bank as a wave of enemy fire crashes in.

Postscript: Supporting fire from our mortars at the patrol base and 105mm guns from Musa Qala soon settled the enemy's hash. We were the able to continue our move without further interference, although it had become too dark for further photography.

The Patrol Base

The Mortar Platoon had arrived ahead of us on the first day by helicopter and was establishing a baseplate position at the patrol base. On its arrival, after the gruelling day-long clash with the enemy, B Company set up bashas and made itself at home. The Mortars were soon busy supporting callsigns on the ground, while the troops carried out personal admin and improved their shelters. The base itself was perched on a hill and manned by a small contingent of ANA. Its exposed position made it a magnet for Taliban indirect fire, and rockets were soon raining down. Thankfully, these fell short, exploding harmlessly in the desert. Over the next few days, the company would mount a series of forays into the surrounding Green Zone, taking the fight to the enemy.

Above left: The mortar crews spring into action and prepare to fire.

Above right: The mortars continue to 'fire for effect', throwing more rounds at the enemy.

This No 1 on the mortar relays mortar using the C2 sight and elevation and deflection drums.

A typical basha set-up, with a sleeping pod and poncho.

Right: An ANA soldier manning the entrance sanger.

Below: Showing the flag for the group photograph.

Dawn Patrol

Stepping off in the hour before dawn, the company mounted another fighting patrol into the Green Zone, the OC determined to take on the insurgents. A rapid cross-country move in darkness brought us to the edge of the inhabited area. We had been engaged from here on the previous day, and a search quickly turned up an empty magazine and spent 7.62 short cases. The troops also recovered a well-used, but functional, Kalashnikov from one of the compounds. Our attached RMP then swabbed some of the locals for powder residue, but the results were clear. The ICOM chatter now suggested the enemy had spotted us and were manoeuvring into position. The men began to deploy, and I joined one of the platoons manning the walls of a nearby compound. From here, they provided overwatch as the rest of the company advanced through the fields and ditches. Both sides then attempted to get into a favourable position, but on this occasion, the enemy failed to engage. Eventually, the decision was made to return to base, which involved an uphill slog across the desert. As we moved into the open, the interpreter informed us the insurgents were trying to set up an RPG shoot, which made things more interesting. We made it back safely, but it was clear the insurgents were still active and willing to take us on.

The troops were not taking any chances after the experience of the previous day's fighting.

Right: **This well-used Kalashnikov was recovered from a local compound, and it was oiled and ready to go.**

Below: **A sniper uses a rooftop perch to search for signs of enemy movement.**

This section leads the advance into the surrounding Green Zone.

Negotiating a water-filled irrigation channel.

Back on dry land. Note the interpreter is travelling light, with just a CamelBak and his ICOM.

A sniper finds himself a good position. Note the size of the L115A2 sniper rifle, which was chambered for the powerful .338 magnum round.

A game of cat and mouse ensued through the fields and ditches.

Breaking out into the open desert area.

The Patrol Home

With the mission winding down, and the Company scheduled to re-deploy, the OC led the men on one last foray into the Green Zone before the return to Musa Qala. It all started quietly enough, and for once it seemed we had caught the enemy napping. Advancing across open fields, the lead section was met with a deluge of automatic fire and a double RPG strike. There followed a furious exchange of fire while mortars were brought down on the enemy position. The company followed up rapidly and it appeared we had the enemy on the back foot. The ICOM confirmed they had taken casualties, and there was an atavistic feeling of having them on the run. Inevitably, things soon bogged down in the tangle of compounds and ditches as the troops attempted to locate and pin down the enemy fighters. Eventually, the OC decided we had reached our limit of exploitation, and we began our move back to the DC at Musa Qala. This was achieved with the platoons leapfrogging each other to guard against the insurgents following up. This was tiring, but effective, and we eventually broke out onto the banks of the Helmand River, with the outline of the DC visible in the distance.

Above left: Shrugging into equipment, this rifleman carries the 40mm rounds for his UGL in leg pouches.

Above right: This rifleman uses a handy ditch as cover. The device attached to the rifle's handguard is a laser designator.

Right: The OC and his radio operator caught behind a low brick wall as the rounds crack in.

Bringing up a ladder to try and get PID (positive identification) on the enemy positions.

The heavily defended DC at Musa Qala.

Exfiltration

After the excitement of the last few days, there was the chance to unwind a little before our move to FOB Edinburgh in the morning. This was via the same fleet of lumbering Mastiff Protected Patrol Vehicles (PPVs) with which we were now familiar. On arrival at the FOB, it turned out that Chinooks were at a premium, which meant a lot of waiting around. Eventually, I was able to catch a flight out with the Mortar Platoon, the big helicopter depositing us back on the pan at Camp Bastion.

Right: The lumbering Mastiffs, each armed with a roof-mounted .50 Browning for local protection.

Below: Taking cover from the Chinook's impressive downdraught.

Left: I follow the last mortarman onto the chopper.

Above: Passing over featureless desert on the flight back to Bastion.

Postscript: The mission to Musa Qala was judged a success, as we had inflicted casualties, and it was reported that the local Taliban commander was 'hiding in the south'. B Company had undoubtedly given the insurgents a run for their money, but the effort could not be sustained, as they were now needed elsewhere.

Kajaki Dam

FOB Kajaki was a name redolent of the Regiment's previous tour in 2006, when it had been the scene of a tragic incident that caused the loss of Corporal Mark Wright in a mine strike. In August, it was to be the focus of the 16 Air Assault Brigade's main effort of the tour. Operation *Oquab Tsuka* (*Eagle's Summit*) would involve escorting a new turbine to the site to bring the dam's hydro-electric plant to full capacity. This would be no mean feat in the face of Taliban resistance, and it would involve two full rifle companies from 3 Para along with other assets. The Combat Logistic Patrol that would carry the dismantled turbine would forge a new route across the desert. This had been discovered by the Pathfinders and would avoid using routes subject to IEDs and insurgent attacks. It turned out the B Company mission to Musa Qala, and a similar operation mounted by A Company to Maiwand, had in fact been part of the deception plan for the mission. With my end-of-tour date now looming, time was short, but it was agreed I would accompany A Company for the initial phase of the operation.

Arrival

A Company was familiar to me from the Kandahar operation, and I joined one of its Chinook flights from KAF, arriving at the dusty LZ above the dam. We were then picked up by Pinzgauers, bumping down the rocky track to the FOB manned by 2 Para. This had the appearance of an old colonial hill station, with a prominent OP perched high on a nearby hill. A suitable compound had already been earmarked for the company and was located a short distance from the dam itself. With the bergens and heavy baggage carried in by Pinzgauers, we set off to walk the two klicks to our new billet. This turned out to be a large and impressive collection of buildings that were well suited for defence. The troops were soon busy building sangers, stripped to the waist and hauling sandbags. Once the work was complete, everyone turned to setting up bashas and heating rations for a meal as the sun finally began to drop on the horizon.

Right: **The troops walk out to their airframes waiting on the pan at KAF.**

Below: **Inside the crowded interior of the Chinook on the flight into Kajaki.**

Above: **One of the well-built bungalows at the FOB.**

Left: **Collecting Bergens carried in by the Pinzgauers.**

Putting the finishing touches to a sanger position.

Setting up cot beds. It was always a bit of a battle to get them together.

Left: The useful discovery of a well.

Below: The compound's thick walls were well suited to defence.

Kajaki Life

The dam complex had originally been constructed by the Americans back in the 1950s, as part of a US aid programme. The area had been the scene of much fighting over the years, and many of the local Afghans had abandoned their homes as a consequence. With the new base established, there was an opportunity to visit the dam for a refreshing swim. The Russians had apparently used Kajaki as an R&R centre, and I could see why. Meanwhile, ANA troops from the Kandak Battalion turned up to support the operation. They occupied a blockhouse close to the entrance to the FOB, which had once been a detention centre for the Russians. It was just as well that we took this fleeting chance for a visit, as things were about to liven up.

Right: A Jackal belonging to the 2 Para Fire Support Group (FSG) at the FOB in Kajaki.

Below: The ANA Kandak arrives to take part in the mission.

Left: This ANA soldier carries a Soviet-made 7.62mm PK machine gun.

Below: The hydro-electric plant attached to the dam.

The remains of an old Russian anti-aircraft gun.

British and ANA soldiers get a lift from a dumpster truck.

Above left: A memorial to the fallen at the Kajaki FOB.

Above right: Things liven up! 2 Para Mortars in action at the FOB.

Below: Additional 105mm Light Guns brought into Kajaki to support the operation.

A Company Contact

The Kandak Battalion were scheduled to make a ground assault on a nearby feature supported by guns and mortars from the Kajaki FOB. Meanwhile, A Company had turned the compound into a firebase and were soon in action after coming under attack from the insurgents. They hammered back with mortar fire as I snapped away with the camera. The baseplates thumped into the earth with every round fired, throwing up clouds of dust. The 105mm Light Guns from Kajaki were soon joining in, plastering the Taliban positions and putting a lid on things. This was to be my last opportunity to capture the action, as I was booked on a helicopter the following morning. In the end, the turbine would be delivered safely, despite the Taliban doing their best to disrupt the operation. They were outnumbered and outgunned.

Right: The Mortar Platoon bed in its weapons; they would soon be needed.

Below: The rooftop OP was a hive of activity.

Above: The Javelin was designed as an anti-tank weapon, but its high trajectory was ideal for engaging compounds.

Below left: The Mortars come into action.

Below right: The impressive muzzle blast as another round is lobbed at the enemy.

The Chinook flight that finally took me out of Kajaki.

Postscript: Operation *Oquab Tsuka* was declared a success at the time, as the new turbine had been successfully delivered to the dam. However, once all the extra troops had withdrawn, the insurgents were soon back, attacking convoys and planting their IEDs. Due to the deteriorating security situation, the contractors and engineers scheduled to carry out the installation never actually got through. As a result, the turbine still lies in its packing crates gathering dust to this day.

End Game

It is now over a decade since I covered the fighting in Helmand and 20 years since the British Army first became engaged in operations in Afghanistan. The US president's decision to finally withdraw from the country brought about a predictable result. With Western support withdrawn, the ANA and its government rapidly collapsed in the face of Taliban advances. I watched the chaotic scenes coming out of Kabul, with a mixture of horror and fascination as thousands of desperate Afghans descended on the international airport. The one positive note I took from the whole debacle was the performance of my own Regiment in carrying out an impossible job under the most trying of circumstances. Historians will judge the wisdom of our precipitate withdrawal from the region but, at this point, I just feel for the families who lost loved ones and the young men who suffered life-changing injuries. Despite this, the men who confronted the Taliban in the fields and ditches of Helmand can still take pride in their achievements. They endured some of the toughest operational conditions British soldiers have encountered since World War Two and took the fight to the enemy.

Utrinque Paratus